Butterfly

Gifts of Wisdom and Laughter from Our Children

Edited by

Mary Ann Casler and Tona Pearce Myers

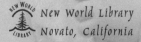 New World Library
Novato, California

New World Library
14 Pamaron Way
Novato, California 94949

Copyright © 2001 by Mary Ann Casler and Tona Pearce Myers

Cover design: Mary Ann Casler
Text design and layout: Mary Ann Casler and Tona Pearce Myers

Library of Congress Cataloging-in-Publication Data
Butterfly kisses : gifts of wisdom and laughter from our children / compiled and edited by Mary Ann Casler and Tona Pearce Myers.
     p. cm.
   ISBN 1-57731-172-8 (cloth : alk. paper)
   1. Children—Quotations. I. Casler, Mary Ann. II. Myers, Tona Pearce, 1966–
PN6328.C5 B88 2001
305.23—dc21   2001016254

First printing, March 2001
ISBN 1-57731-172-8
Printed in Canada on acid-free, recycled paper
Distributed to the trade by Publishers Group West

10 9 8 7 6 5 4 3 2

To our children, Sydney, Jacob,
Taylor, and Jared.
They have taught us so much.

CONTENTS

ACKNOWLEDGMENTS

We wish to thank our families and especially our children, Sydney, Jacob, Taylor, and Jared. May they continue to share their wisdom with equal abandon all their lives. A special thanks to our husbands, Dave and Dutch, for their support and childcare efforts during the completion of this book.

Our sincere thanks go to all the people at New World Library: Marc Allen, Cathy Bodenmann, Dean Campbell, Victoria Williams-Clarke, Katie Farnam Conolly, Marjorie Conte, Jason Gardner, Paul Haas, Georgia Hughes, Katie Karavolos, Munro Magruder, Gina Misiroglu, Monique Muhlenkamp, and Christina Silveira.

We would also like to thank Dede Bassi of Rancho Elementary; Kelly Carlson of Good Shepherd; and Kersten Miller and Melissa Souza of Creekside Village Preschool for their superb assistance in inspiring their students to be a part of this compilation.

It is also important for us to thank Lindsay Stevens for her excellent artwork and willingness to draw and color until all our hearts were content.

Thanks to Thom Rollerson of the Dream Foundation for being who he is and for granting extraordinary wishes to terminally ill adults and their families.

INTRODUCTION

While putting this book together there was a story that was circulating on the Internet about a father and daughter. It was a heartwarming story that represented why we were interested in doing this book. It shows that we often learn the most from our children.

Some time ago, a father punished his three-year-old daughter for wasting a roll of gold wrapping paper. Money was tight, and he became infuriated when she tried to decorate a box to put under the tree.

Nevertheless, she brought the gift to her father the next morning and said, "This is for you, Daddy." He was embarrassed by his earlier overreaction, but his anger flared again when he found that the box was empty. He said to her, "Don't you know that when you give someone a present, there's supposed to be something inside of it?" His daughter looked up at him with tears in her eyes and said, "Oh, Daddy it's not empty. I blew kisses into the box. They are all for you."

The father was crushed. He put his arms around his daughter and he begged her forgiveness.

He kept that gold box by his bed for years. Whenever he was discouraged, he would take out an imaginary kiss and remember the love of his child who had put it there.

In a very real sense, each of us as parents has been given a golden container filled with unconditional love and kisses from our children. There is no more precious possession anyone could hold.

Children have a wonderment and wisdom that many times we adults overlook. It is this wisdom and delight that we tried to capture with the children's thoughts in this book. Most expressions were actually written by the children themselves. Some of the stories have a small explanation from the parent to help clarify the situation in which the particular child spoke or acted.

Some of the stories will touch your hearts; others will tickle your funny bone. In choosing these thoughts we have tried to convey the incredible variety of wisdom that children have to share. If we can slow down a bit and listen to the children there will surely be some gifts passed between the generations.

— Mary Ann Casler
and Toni Pearce Myers

IF WiSHES WERE TRUE & DREAMS BECAME REAL

I wish we could send all the bad people to the moon. Then everywhere would be as nice as my house.

— Michael, age 6

I want to be a policeman when I grow up. Then I would put all the bad guys in jail. Jail isn't a happy place. All the bad guys are mean to each other and they don't get to go outside and play. Maybe we should let all the bad guys play outside a lot with us kids and it will make them happy. Then we can let them out of jail and they will be good guys again.

— Theo, age 4

3

If I could have anything in the world I would like a dragon. The dragon would be nice and I could fly anywhere in the world with my family. My Dad and Mom deserve a vacation and I could take them anywhere with my dragon.

— Garrett, age 5

4

Dear Santa,

I was hoping you would do some things this Christmas. Please help there to be no crime against people's beliefs and disbeliefs. And the one thing I would like is another hamster that looks like the one I had before who died.

— Kyle, age 8

5

Dear Santa,

I would like for teenagers not to get addicted to drugs and for all people to be kind to each other. For me I would like something for my hair like barrettes. Don't bother if you can't get me anything, though. It will be all right.

— Ali, age 9

Dear Mom and Dad,

This year for Hanukkah I would like you to help out with some things. Please try to stop diseases from getting worse. Please put up tables of food and clothing that poor people could have for free every month. For me, just a little thing would be great.

— Allison, age 9

7

My DREAM would be . . .

There are many places in this world
Some that I have been to
and some that I have not,
Some that I may never see.
This world is very big indeed,
big enough that there will be
places I will never see.

— Chad, age 12

8

LIONS & TIGERS & BEARS

Why my D☀G is my best friend . . .

I was playing outside one day when I was four. My mom had gone inside to get a snack for me and my dog Nacoma. While Mom was inside I jumped in our baby pool head first. I don't remember anything after that but my mom told me the whole story. What she told me is this.

I knocked myself out by hitting my head on the ground — kind of like going to sleep. I started to drink the water into my body and began to drown. My dog started barking and scratching at the back door. Mom opened the door and yelled for her to stop!

She didn't see me — Nacoma raced over to the pool and my mom followed and found me. The ambulance came and took me to the hospital where I had to stay a few days.

After that I went home and from that day on Nacoma was allowed to sleep in bed with me. Beacuse I love my dog so much — she protects and loves me back.

— Bradley, age 9

You can tell animals come from God just like babies because they smell good and they shine.

— Chloe, age 5

12

I admire my dog because when I fall down she always comes up to me and makes me feel warm and happy and like playing again. I love Claire.

— Patrick, age 9

13

I want to be an animal mother when I grow up because I want to take care of all the homeless animals and show them what a family is.

14

— Kaitlin, age 7

When dogs die they go to the clouds. The clouds are giant dog biscuits and they can have as much as they want.

— Jessica, age 5

15

When we were leaving to go to the movies an injured duck crossed in front of our car. My son's ten-year-old friend quickly said, "I know that duck, I saw it yesterday and tried to catch it."

"I really think he needs help," he told me. "I am going to try to catch him again."

After watching for a moment and seeing how important it was to him, I agreed. Within seconds, he jumped out, swooped up the duck, and quickly tucked him under his arm. We watched, amazed.

We decided to make a quick detour to our local shelter in hopes of saving our new friend. At the shelter the children kissed the duck and wished their new friend, Quackers, a speedy recovery.

After returning to the car I asked Andrew why it was so important to him to help the duck.

"My mom always told me that we are supposed to help people in trouble. And that it is especially important to help those in your neighborhood. I just suppose she meant ducks too, especially those that live near you."

— Andrew, age 10

17

I love trees. Trees are strong enough for me to climb, big enough for me to sit under, pretty enough for me to look at, and happy enough to make me smile. I hope everybody loves trees.

— Felicia, age 6

Rainbows are made up of sun and all the colors there are. Rainbows follow you when you are driving because they have wheels on the ends of their bows and the wind blows them to you. Then you can always see the rainbow until all the sun goes away.

— Brittany, age 7

I admire Garfield the cat because he is funny and he acts the way you would if it was okay.

— Evan, age 9

SCHOOL DAYS

On the first day of kindergarten my son, Michael, was very excited to go to school. His father, who worked nights, walked him the three blocks from our house to his new class. After kissing him good-bye my husband walked home to go to sleep. At 12:30 I got a call from the school principal. My son was missing. I raced to school, my heart wrenched, thinking the worst. He was nowhere to be found. The teacher said that she was getting everyone ready to lie down for their naps and the next thing she knew he was gone. The police were called and I went home to wake my husband. I ran into the house and opened the bedroom door. There lying in

the bed under my husband's arm was my way-
ward son, sound asleep.

I woke Michael and asked him how he got
there. Michael replied, "Mama, the teacher said
we had to lie down for our naps. I couldn't get to
sleep and I always nap with Daddy. So I came
home. It feels so much better to sleep here."

— Michael, age 5

23

I got really scared. Then my heart got scared. It started running up into my throat and I thought it would fall on the floor.

— Kramer, age 5
about the first day of school

I was celebrating my birthday with some of the children from the class I teach. After singing "Happy Birthday" to me the class got quiet. One little girl came up and asked, "How old are you?"

I replied, "I just turned fifty."

"Wow, you'd think you'd be dead by now," she replied.

— Isabel,
a pre-school teacher

While carpooling the children in my neighborhood to school one Wednesday morning, I pulled into the parking lot to do my daily drop-off. My oldest rider, Andrew, ten years old, suddenly realized he had forgotten his trumpet. He sat where he was, arms crossed. I was due at work in five minutes, right at the time he was expected at school. I pulled to the side of the parking lot and tried to phone some neighbors to bring Andrew his trumpet, to no avail.

"Andrew, why don't you share a trumpet with someone?" I asked.

Andrew replied, "I'm not getting out! If I go in without my trumpet they will send me to singing class." He began to cry.

"If I go back to get your trumpet you will be

late for school and get a pink slip and so will I."

He replied, "I don't care if I get a pink slip. You can write me a note and I will write one for you and then it will be okay."

I decided to go get his trumpet. Unfortunately, the traffic was worse than usual, and it took us more than thirty minutes. At last our mission was accomplished, and Andrew had his trumpet and was back at school.

The next morning I did my normal pick-up and Andrew was standing in his driveway holding a bouquet of flowers and a card.

The card read:

"I'm sorry I forgot my trumpet. I know I wasted your work time, and I'll make it up for you next Wednesday. I will have my backpack glued to my trumpet case. If that happens again you can just forget me. Thank you so, so much."

— Andrew, age 10

HOUSE OF GOD

My mother is very religious. She goes to play bingo at church every week even if she has a cold.

— Annette, age 9

I think a lot more people would go to church if it was moved to Disneyland.

— Loreen, age 9

One day I saw Sean playing with the mailbox we have at church. I asked him what he was doing. As children do, he answered my question with a question: "Is this where God gets his mail?"

I replied, "I don't think so."

"Why? Did he move? I just prayed to him and how will he get my message?"

— Sean, age 4

31

During a baptism service we were attending, my three-year-old son was curious about the devotional candle offerings burning around the outer walls of the church. I took him to the offerings enclave and explained to him that when people were sick or needed help someone would light a candle and pray for them. God would try to help them.

We took our places in the pews as more people arrived. A frail elderly woman pulling an oxygen tank walked in late. The woman sat behind us in the pew and my son's interest in her never wavered throughout the ceremony.

Afterwards, my son turned to me and said,

"Momma, that lady is really sick. She needs some help. Can we light a candle for her?"

— Taylor, age 3

It was Christmastime. My son was attending Christian school and for two whole weeks he carried a present to and from school every day. Finally I asked him why he kept taking this present back and forth to school everyday. He replied, "I am trying to figure out how to give it to God for his birthday on Christmas."

The pastor told him he thought it would be okay to leave it on the altar for God. Jacob ran to the church and placed the present on the altar. A smile came over his face and he sang "Happy Birthday" to God.

— Jacob, age 4

WHAT DOES GOD DO ALL DAY?

I think God wears all the love everyone gives Him.

— *Nicole*, age 12

God did not make cigarettes or cigars.

— *Alexandra*, age 6

"Look! A jet airplane. It's flying higher into the sky and taking all the dead people to heaven. I bet the boss of all the dead people is flying it."

— Rory, age 4

God is clean. God's clothes are white. That way He blends into the clouds. That's why we can't see Him and we have to be good all the time because He might be standing right next to you.

— Ryan, age 5

There is a God because people need Him.

— Michael, age 9

L ate one night, several hours after putting my six-year-old daughter to bed, I heard her stirring in her room. I quietly went in her room and asked her if she was okay. She seemed to be sad and concerned about something. I asked her what had awakened her. She looked at me with sad eyes and said, "Mommy, I'm beginning to forget."

"What are you beginning to forget?" I asked her. Her reply stunned me.

"I'm beginning to forget when I was with God, before I came here, and it makes me very sad."

— Mia, age 6

40

It's God's job to catch all the bad guys and throw them to the sharks and then the sharks eat them. The bad guys then turn into sharks. That's why sharks and bad guys are mean.

— Walton, age 4

I know that God loves everybody, but He never
met my sister.

— Arnold, age 4

41

Evan: Mommy, where does God live?
Mommy: He lives in our hearts.
Evan: Then, I don't think I should eat my oatmeal
because I am afraid I will get His face all dirty.

— Evan, age 4
a conversation while eating breakfast

42

I wish God had a big bucket of glitter. If He did, He could pour it out when it rains and we could have silver glitter in the rain. That way we would never have any more bad flooding and nobody would lose their homes.

43

— Jake, age 5

I bet it's very hard for God to love all the people in the world. There are only four people in my family and I can never do it.

— George, age 6

44

HEAVEN
& PRAYERS

I like heaven. I go there sometimes when I sleep to visit my daddy. He gives me hugs and kisses and tells me stories so that I sleep good all night long.

— Cody, age 6

Heaven is all full of souls.

— Christa, age 3

Heaven has no dark time. But when it's dark time on earth the angels come down from heaven to help the babies come out of people's tummies. And then we have a new baby.

— Jacob, age 6

Heaven must be like...a fun place that has games and church and has school once a week.

— Sydney, age 9

Thank you for Mommy and Daddy, Memaw and Papaw, pretty big-girls underwear, and everybody in the world.

— Cassandra, age 4
during nightly prayers

Mean people get a little bit of heaven. It's not quite as nice as other parts of heaven. Good people get lots of heaven with beautiful days and happy nights. Everyone gets some heaven because inside everybody has some good parts.

— Alan, age 9

I think in heaven everything is made of clouds. I think whenever you fall or trip a cloud appears and you do not get hurt or hit your butt hard because even the furniture is made of clouds.

— Nick, age 9

50

J. D.: Mommy, what was Grandma's favorite color?
Mom: Red.
J. D.: I knew it — because Grandma is living in heaven in a big red house and she is real happy!

— J. D., age 5
after the death of his grandmother

Angels live far away downtown. They talk Italian.

— Alessia, age 4

52

I would like to go to heaven someday because I know my brother won't be there.

— Stephen, age 8

Dear God,

It rained for our whole vacation and my father is mad! He said some things that people are not supposed to say, but I hope you will not hurt him anyway.

Sincerely,

Your friend
(but I'm not going to tell you who I am)

— Zach, age 8

53

When I talk to God I pray and I can't say any bad words.

— Sean, age 8

Dear God,

Are there any devils on earth? I think there may be one in my class.

— Salina, age 10

Dear God,

If you watch me in church on Sunday, I'll show you my new shoes.

— Cathy, age 5

55

Dear God,

Thank you for my baby brother, but what I prayed for was a puppy.

— Alex, age 6

Dear God,

Instead of letting people die and having to make new ones, why don't you just keep the ones you have now?

— Sienna, age 7

Dear God,

Please pray for all the airline pilots. I am flying to California tomorrow.

— Laurie, age 10

FRIENDS
ARE...

A friend can be nice to you on the outside but really mean on the inside. I had a friend like that once — I'm not gonna tell her name because that would make me mean.

— Kaitlen, age 9

The qualities of a good friend blossom from the heart. A good friend should always be there and grow old with you.

— Sydney, age 9

60

Someone who is selfish and unfair is not a good friend. Friends don't have to have a lot of money and dress up everyday, they just have to have a good soul.

— Sandy, age 10

Dear Lindsay,

You are such a good friend. I learned how to sing the ABCs from you. You always say you're sorry when you hurt my feelings or if you do anything bad. So I have some advice for you: never talk back to grown-ups, always help people, never kick or punch anyone, and always be careful. You may want to do the splits — but I wouldn't because I don't want you to hurt yourself.

Love, your friend Shelley
age 7

It doesn't matter what a friend looks like on the outside as long as they are beautiful on the inside.

— Royan, age 10

BOYS & GIRLS

64

Jack and Jill went up the hill to fetch a pail of water. Jack wanted to carry the pail, but Jill was a big, strong girl and didn't need any help. Jack fell down the hill and Jill carried the pail all the way back without any help from Jack.

— Chelsea, age 5
her version of her favorite nursery rhyme

Girls . . .
go to college to get more knowledge.
Boys . . .
go to Mars to get more candy bars.

— Jimmy, age 7

Girls . . .
go to the sun because
it is way more fun.
Boys . . .
play on the moon
because they don't
have to come home so
soon.

— Annette, age 6

The Old Nursery Rhyme Goes...

Girls are made of
sugar and spice and everything nice.
Boys are made of
snips and snails and puppy dog tails.

The New Nursery Rhyme Is...

Girls are made of
the color pink, Barbie dolls, and Tootsie Rolls.
Boys are made of
Sweet Tarts, trucks, and baseball games.

— Amanda, age 8

Girls change their minds so much. I think girls change their minds so much because they like to and they don't know what else to say.

— Jared, age 7

Shelley: Yuck, Mommy, why did you do that?
Mommy: Because I love him.
Shelley: Well, I know you love him, but that doesn't mean you have to kiss him!

— Shelley, age 8
after seeing her mother and father kiss

NEW ARRIVALS & FAMILY

I was pregnant with my second child. My daughter Maggie was very excited about having a little brother or sister. She began to cuddle with her dolls and pat my stomach in anticipation of the new addition to our family.

After a few months Maggie became convinced that she too was pregnant and a baby was growing in her tummy. She became bothersome about certain things, such as not wanting to get dressed because her clothes would be too tight and hurt the baby in her tummy. This went on for quite a few weeks with me becoming more agitated about her behavior.

One day she wouldn't take a bath. According to her the water would scare our baby. I explained to her again that she didn't have a baby inside her stomach. She began to throw a tantrum and refused to get in the tub. I grabbed her under the arms and began to lift her into the tub.

"Mommy, you are hurting my baby!" Maggie yelled adamantly.

At this point I was completely exhausted and emotionally drained and began to cry. Maggie looked up at me as sweetly as only she can and said, "Mama, don't cry. It's okay. I know I don't really have a baby in my tummy, but I thought we could share. That way you wouldn't get too tired and I could help a little."

— Maggie, age 4

My baby sister needs a little baby spoon to eat. It's really tiny. When she cries her mouth is so much bigger than when she eats.

— Margaret, age 4

During my second pregnancy my four-year-old son took it upon himself to talk and sing to his new baby sister. He continued to do this throughout the whole nine months. After our daughter was born with severe medical problems we were faced with having to tell our son his sister might not stay with us. Our son immediately stressed to us that he must go see her. We reluctantly agreed and arranged for him to visit her in the pediatric intensive care unit. We feared it might frighten him.

He went directly to her small bassinett and began talking and singing the songs he had sung while I was pregnant. The next day she took a turn for the better and went on to make a miraculous recovery. Our son makes sure anyone who comes to visit is well informed on how he talked his new sister into getting better and coming to stay with us at our house.

— Jonathan, age 5

73

*A*n aunt eavesdropped on the following scene between cousins: "Why are you sitting on the stairs, Chelsea? Don't you want to come and watch a video?"

"No, I want to be with my mom."

"Where's your mom?"

"She's with Kimberly. She's always with Kimberly now."

Sniffles. Chelsea seems to be crying a little.

"It really makes me mad. I need her, too. She's my mom but the baby gets her all to herself."

"I know just what you mean. But don't worry. Your mom loves you, too. She loves you just as much as she always did, and since you're a bigger girl you don't need her as much as Kimberly needs her right now. Since you're bigger, you can take care of yourself and Kimberly can't, so you have to let Kimberly have your mom all the time. But pretty soon it won't be like that anymore. When Christopher was born, I was really sad because my mom spent all her time with him. He was a big crybaby and I didn't like him. Then, I found out that Mom still spent time with me and I got to play with Christopher, too. Pretty soon, you'll be happy that you have a sister. You'll get to help dress her and play with her and share with her. A sister and a mom are better than just a mom. Wait and see."

— Kammeron, age 5, and Chelsea, age 3

I want to be a mom when I grow up just like my mom. I will be nice, caring, loving, and I will know everything because all mommies know the answer for everything.

— Jessica, age 5

Families are important because mothers and dads do everything. Mothers always do everything but not fathers because they just sit and watch TV.

— Frank, age 5

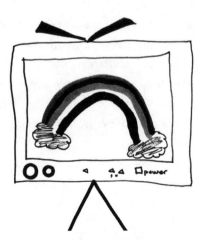

Sometimes children say the funniest things. I was pregnant with my second child. It was the evening of the due date. When I went to my four-year-old son's preschool to pick him up they were in the middle of snack time. I bent down to help a child clean his hands when my water broke. When I say broke I really mean burst. Within seconds there was a puddle beneath me and labor had started. All the children were asking what was wrong with me, including my son. I told them that nothing was wrong but that the baby was coming and we had to go home quickly. My son skipped to the car and watched as I waddled along. Within the five minutes it took to get home I had another couple of contractions and was getting pretty worried. My son started to get agitated at my distress and I couldn't answer him when he asked, "What's wrong, Mama?"

When we arrived home my son ran into the house where his grandfather was waiting and yelled, "The baby is coming out, and Mama peed her pants on purpose."

— Taylor, age 4

I'm good at sports. I guess I get that from my dad. My dad is pretty smart. I guess he gets that from me.

— T. J., age 5

HOW DO I *LOVE* THEE?

One evening as our family was snuggling in bed, my young daughter looked very sweetly at me and her father and said, "I am so glad that I picked you for my parents. You know, you get to pick who your mom and dad will be before you come here, and I am just really glad that I picked you."

— Samantha, age 6

One day, as I was picking my daughter up from school, she said to me, "Mom, why do we have two arms?" and I replied, "So we can give great big hugs."

Sabrina thought this over and said, "Well, then how come we don't have three arms?" "Well, why would you want three arms?" I asked. "Because then I could give you bigger hugs that feel three arms bigger!"

— Sabrina, age 4

Families are important because they have a certain way to love you that no one else can.

— Courtney, age 9

Taylor: I have special powers to see behind me.
Mom: I wish I had special powers.
Taylor: You do, mom.
Mom: What are my special powers?
Taylor: You have special powers in your heart to
love me.

— Taylor, age 4

One morning after spending the night at a new friend's house, I was awakened by her two young boys whom I had never met. My friend had insisted I sleep in her bed while she slept on the sofa. Her boys crawled over me and showered me with hugs and kisses before I was even able to tell them who I was.

"I love you," purred the older boy. I pulled the covers down from over my face. Both boys sat up straight, studied my sleepy face, and said in unison: "You're not my mommy!"

I laughed and said, "No, I'm not. Your mommy is in the family room." They looked at each other, pounced on top of me, and squealed, "That's okay! We love you anyway!"

— Richard, age 7, and James, age 5

When people wave at me they turn my round, brown eyes into hearts.

— Parker, age 4

Mama, you look so nice. God painted you well.

— Austin, age 4
while watching
his mom get ready
to go out

Love is cold sometimes when people are not nice. But when people are nice love feels warm and happy.

— Natalie, age 5

"You don't smile very much," Angie said to my boyfriend while at the park with some friends. And it was true. He didn't.

"I bet I could make you smile," she said.

"Think so?" he replied.

"Oh, yes!" she clapped.

For a couple of minutes she danced around and made silly faces, told knock-knock jokes, and then finally collapsed on the ground glowing and satisfied.

"I did it!" she said triumphantly.

My boyfriend looked at her squarely and said, "But I didn't smile."

"Oh yes you did!" she exclaimed. "You smiled

with your eyes. They were full of love and smiles and you can't turn that off like you can turn the one on your face off."

— Angie, age 6

91

Valentine's Day is important because you give your hearts away to people you love and they feel bubbly.

— Molly, age 5

MARRIAGE & RELATIONSHIPS

My family is broken like my bike when the tires
go flat. It still works but it's slower and bumpier.

— Anessa, age 11
about her parents' divorce

Dates are for having fun and people should use them to get to know each other. Even boys have something to say if you listen long enough.

— Lynne, age 9

95

The rule goes like this: If you kiss someone, then you should marry them and have kids with them. It's the right thing to do.

— Bryan, age 8

While having lunch with my young friend, Katy, we noticed a couple behind us having an argument. This prompted her to remark that her own parents, whom I knew to be having marital problems, didn't get along so well either.

"I wish they would let me teach them how to get along with each other. But they won't listen to me," she shrugged.

"You think you could help them?" I asked.

"Yes, I would," she replied confidently. "Because I'm little. You see, the littler you are, the more you know. Little babies know everything and when you get older you get stupider and stupider.

"It's sad they fight, but they are old and stupid and they can't help it."

— Katy, age 6

Married people usually look happy to talk to other people.

— Eddie, age 5

It's better for girls to be single but not for boys. Boys need someone to clean up after them.

— Anita, age 9

No person really decides before they grow up who they're going to marry. God decides it all way before, and you get to find out later who you're stuck with.

— Kirsten, age 10

CHILLY THOUGHTS

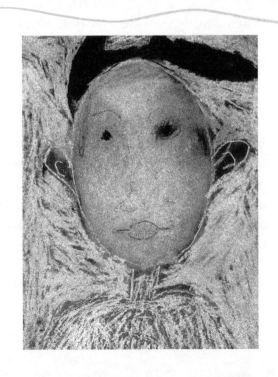

When Daddy gets mad he gets bigger and bigger and bigger, then he's as big as the whole room.

— Joseph, age 3

Peter is a magician. He is really calm. If someone doesn't pay him, he won't yell. He'll go into a room that will give him privacy and use his anger there. He is talented too. He can make an old plant alive and he can make a cloudy sky a sunny day.

— Graham, age 8

That guy is a scary guy. If he would shave off all his hair, cut his beard, and get butt naked he wouldn't scare me anymore.

— David, age 3
about a stranger

It makes me sad when people hit me because it hurts outside and inside too.

— Jake, age 7

My brain hurts when people yell. The words get caught in my head and bounce around like a Superball. Then I get one big ache up there.

— Connor, age 7

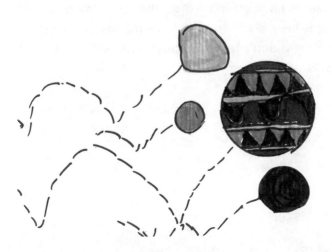

It stinks. It really, really stinks. The only time I feel normal is when I am at camp with all the other kids with AIDS. Every year we come back together. It is really happy to see everyone, but really sad too, because some of the kids don't make it till the next year. The best thing about that is they don't have to take the meds anymore, and they don't feel sick anymore. But all in all it just really stinks.

— Nikolaus, age 8
about having AIDS

IF I RULED THE WORLD

If I were president of the United States I would change all of the gun factories into learning factories. That way we would have smart people instead of mean people.

— Dimitri, age 9

If I were in charge of the world I would make it okay to spit in public because it is fun and I am good at it.

— Jimmy, age 7

Taylor: Why do you have to vote?

Mom: Because we have to choose a new president.

Taylor: What's a president do?

Mom: He's the boss of the whole country. I want one person to win, and Daddy wants the other one to win.

Taylor: There's only two! You'd think more than two people would like to do that job.

— Taylor, age 5

If I were president I would make more hamburgers so nobody would be hungry.

— Leslie, age 5
while waiting for dinner

If I were president of the country I would pass a law that all the kids would have school outside because I think they would learn better and the teachers would be happier and more excited about what they were teaching.

109

— Katie, age 10

If I ruled the world, everything would be pink and purple with sparkles and would glow in the dark.

— Cassie, age 4

WHAT I'VE *LEARNED* SO FAR

While attending a sidewalk art show my daughter taught me a very powerful lesson.

We were walking by the beautiful chalk drawings on the sidewalk. She loved the colors and the paintings of animals. At one chalk painting I stopped and said, "Look, honey, there's an Indian girl," as I pointed to a Native American girl in traditional dress.

My daughter asked, "Where, Momma?"

"Right there," I replied, pointing again.

"Momma, all I see is a beautiful little girl."

— Cassie, age 4

Go to the bathroom before you go to bed. Don't pet dogs that you don't know. Laugh at your baby brother and he will laugh, too. Always say good night because it makes you sleep better.

— Charlie, age 5

When you wake up, smile first thing, then your day will be happier. Pick up all the things you play with or they might get lost, and most important, don't drink the bathwater because my mom says it will make you sick.

— Cassie, age 5

Knowledge is written. Wisdom is within. Intelligence is knowledge and wisdom that have been passed to you.

— Jordana, age 9

Don't put your fingers in your nose, it will bleed. Don't put money in your mouth, because I swallowed a quarter once. Don't hit people or call them names because it hurts. Tell a big person if you see a gun or a fire. The couch is for sitting not for jumping, but Mommy lets me do it when Daddy's not home.

— Tyler, age 4

If you lie down with dogs they might fall asleep on your lap. Sing and the world will jump for joy. Don't bite the hand that feeds you, it might bite back. You can't teach an old dog any tricks. A penny saved is so, so lucky!

— Michaela, age 7

I am going to tell you some things. Don't do drugs, don't ever play with fire, and always wear a helmet when you ride your bike.

— Kelley, age 7

My family and I were driving to Canada for vacation. When we entered Canada my husband and I got out of the car to take the customary photo at the "Welcome to Canada" sign. My youngest daughter looked from the sign on the Canadian side to the similar sign on the United States side of the border.

Confused, Marina looked up at me and said, "Mom, there's no difference between here and there, and there is no difference between us and them."

I said, "I know, honey."

She replied, "I think it's the same all over the world and we should probably just have one big country."

— Marina, age 8

My dad told me the world was round like a ball.
I don't believe it, though, because if it were like
a ball everyone would fall off when it bounced.

— Ray, age 5

120

Dear Jakey,

I have learned a lot since I was younger and I would like to tell you a couple of things. Never talk back, always raise your hand before you talk in school, never be mean to anyone, always help others, and much more. I have learned a lot more things but don't have room to list them all. I will tell you always and maybe you can learn from some of the things I've learned before you make a mistake. You can always come and ask me if you are not sure. You will always be my younger brother.

— Syd, age 10

R espect other people

E mpty my milk glass in the morning

S how respect

P oliteness is better than rudeness

O nly you can bring up your grades

N ever talk when someone else is

S ay thank you — always

I gnore bullies

B e a good friend to everyone

I gnore bad people's behavior

L ive honestly

I mpress your teachers and parents

T ry your best

Y awn before bed.

— Compiled by Rancho Elementary, grade 4

122

ETCETERA

ABOUT THE
EDITORS

Mary Ann Casler is a graduate of the Academy of Art College of San Francisco, where she majored in graphic design. She has won three Addy Awards for excellence in design. Her undergraduate work included child psychology, bereavement, and elementary school education. She has worked for the Marin Humane Society, Marin Productions, and has been a freelance designer. Currently she is the art director at New World Library. She is the mother of two wonderful children and makes her home in Northern California.

Tona Pearce Myers holds a bachelor's degree in creative writing from Sonoma State University. She is a published poet and has contributed articles to such publications as *Mothering* magazine and *The Mandala*. She is the editor of *The Soul of Creativity: Insights into the Creative Process*. She has worked in publishing and the book industry for more than fifteen years. She is currently the production manager at New World Library. She is a proud mother of two boys and lives in Marin County, California.

ABOUT THE

DREAM FOUNDATION

In April 1994, Thomas Rollerson's partner, Timothy Palmer, was diagnosed with a catastrophic illness. When Timm expressed a final wish, Thomas phoned a wish-granting agency for children, and discovered that no such organization existed for adults. Thomas found a way to grant Timm's final wish, and shortly after Timm passed away in the summer of 1994, Thomas created the Dream Foundation with the support of his community and friends to honor Timm's spirit.

The mission of the Dream Foundation is to grant final wishes to terminally ill adults with special dreams they would like to fullfill before their deaths, but who lack the resources to realize their dreams.

127

ABOUT THE
ILLUSTRATIONS

We would like to thank all the young artists who helped to bring life to this book through their drawings. Their sincere effort and creativity shines through each and every image.

Graham, age 8
99

Jacob, age 7
17, 45, 50, 83, 91, 92, 93, 114, 116

Lindsay, age 7
xii, 1, 4, 6, 8, 11, 29, 34, 52, 59,
65, 72, 88, 103, 108, 112, 124, 125, 129

Michelle, age 12
37

Sydney, age 10
**21, 25, 27, 33, 45, 47, 55,
63, 77, 105, 111**

Sandy, age 9
9, 29, 35, 57, 69

Katie, age 7
18

Rancho Elementary, 4th grade
81

129